POUNCING BOBCATS

by Joelle Riley

↳ Lerner Publications Company • Minneapolis

For Kiran

This book is available in two editions:
Library binding by Lerner Publications Company, a division of Lerner Publishing Group
Soft cover by First Avenue Editions, an imprint of Lerner Publishing Group
241 First Avenue North
Minneapolis, MN 55401 U.S.A.

Website address: www.lernerbooks.com

Words in *italic type* are explained in a glossary on page 30.

Library of Congress Cataloging-in-Publication Data

Riley, Joelle.
    Pouncing bobcats / by Joelle Riley.
        p. cm. — (Pull ahead books)
    Summary: Simple text and photographs introduce the
    physical characteristics, behavior, and habitat of bobcats.
    ISBN: 0–8225–0686–6 (lib. bdg. : alk. paper)
    ISBN: 0–8225–0965–2 (pbk. bdg. : alk. paper)
    1. Bobcat—Juvenile literature. [1. Bobcat.]
I. Title. II. Series.
QL737.C23 R55 2003
599.75'36—dc21   2001005482

Manufactured in the United States of America
1 2 3 4 5 6 — JR — 08 07 06 05 04 03

What animal is hiding in this tree?

This animal is a bobcat.

A bobcat looks like a big house cat
with a short, stubby tail.
But bobcats are wild animals.

A bobcat has a furry *ruff* around its face.

Its ears have furry *tufts* that stick straight up.

A bobcat's fur is tan
or reddish brown.

It is covered
with dark
spots.

This bobcat
is cleaning
its fur.

The bobcat
uses its
rough
tongue to
lick away
dirt.

Bobcats can live in
many kinds of places.

Some
bobcats
live in dry
deserts.

Some live in forests
or grassy places.

Other bobcats live
in mountains or swamps.

Bobcats are graceful.

They are good at keeping
their balance.

Bobcats are also good climbers.

How does a bobcat
hold onto a tree?

A bobcat has sharp
claws on its paws.

The bobcat
uses its
claws to
hold tight
to a tree's
bark.

Bobcats have sharp teeth, too.

A bobcat uses its claws and teeth
to hunt for food.

Bobcats usually hunt small animals such as rabbits, mice, and birds.

The animals a bobcat hunts are called its *prey.*

Sometimes bobcats hunt deer.
But hunting deer is hard.

A deer is much bigger
than a bobcat.

Bobcats wait quietly for prey
to come near.

They can sit still for a long time.

Look!
An animal is coming!

Bobcats can see small movements.
They can hear tiny noises.

This bobcat sees an animal.
It sneaks toward the prey.

Creep, creep. Sneaking up on prey
is called *stalking*.

POUNCE! A bobcat catches
its prey by jumping on top of it.

What does a bobcat do when it
catches its prey?

First the bobcat looks
around carefully.

Other animals might want
to take its prey.

Then the bobcat finds a safe place to eat its prey.

Why else do bobcats need a safe place?

A mother bobcat needs a
safe place to hide her babies.

Baby bobcats are called *kittens*.
The kittens' home is called a *den*.

A mother bobcat takes
good care of her kittens.

She watches
to make
sure her
kittens do
not get hurt.

As bobcat kittens get older,
they begin to explore.

They learn
how to
climb trees.

WAP! Bobcat kittens love to play with their brothers and sisters.

The kittens wrestle together.
They chase bugs.

When kittens play,
they are learning how to hunt prey.

Playing helps kittens grow up
to be pouncing bobcats!

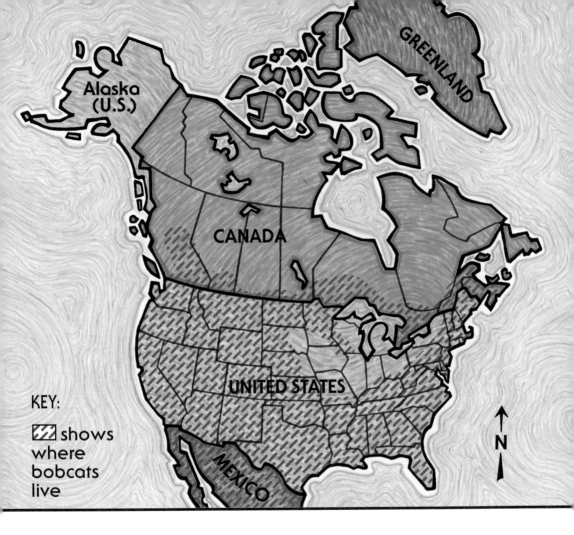

KEY:

▨ shows where bobcats live

Find your state or province on this map.
Do bobcats live near you?

Parts of a Bobcat's Body

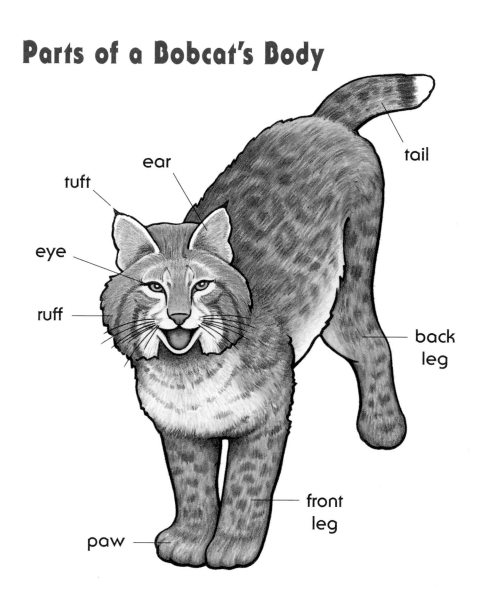

tail

ear

tuft

eye

ruff

back leg

front leg

paw

Glossary

den: a safe place where baby bobcats live

kittens: baby bobcats

prey: the animals that a bobcat hunts and eats

ruff: long fur around a bobcat's face

stalking: sneaking up on an animal

tufts: the furry tips of a bobcat's ears

Hunt and Find

- bobcats **climbing** on pages 11–12
- a bobcat's **den** on page 22
- a bobcat's **fur** on pages 5–7
- bobcats **hunting** on pages 13–19
- bobcat **kittens** on pages 22–27
- a bobcat **pouncing** on page 19

About the Author

Joelle Riley grew up in Pennsylvania, where she knew all of the pet cats in her neighborhood. She loved to watch their graceful movements as they climbed trees and pounced on leaves and bugs. Now she lives in Minnesota with two cats, Boomer and Ceili, and two greyhounds, Wave and Buddy.

Photo Acknowledgments

The photographs in this book are reproduced with permission from: © Alan & Sandy Carey, pp. 3, 5, 9, 11, 12, 13, 17, 19, 22, 25, 31; © Robert Winslow, pp. 4, 6, 7, 8, 10, 14, 15, 16, 20, 21, 23, 24, 26, 27; © Michael P. Turco, p. 18. Cover © Robert Winslow.